Kid Pickers

HOW TO TURN JUNK INTO TREASURE

MIKE WOLFE

WITH **Lily Sprengelmeyer**

ILLUSTRATIONS BY **Mike Right**

Feiwel and Friends

NEW YORK

A Feiwel and Friends Book
An Imprint of Macmillan

Feiwel and Friends books may be purchased for business or promotional use.
For information on bulk purchases, please contact the Macmillan Corporate
and Premium Sales Department at (800) 221-7945 x5442 or by e-mail
at specialmarkets@macmillan.com.

Library of Congress Cataloging-in-Publication Data Available

ISBN: 978-1-250-00848-0 (hardcover)
1 3 5 7 9 10 8 6 4 2

ISBN: 978-1-250-01930-1 (paperback)
1 3 5 7 9 10 8 6 4 2

ISBN: 978-1-250-00849-7 (ebook)

Book design by April Ward

Feiwel and Friends logo designed by Filomena Tuosto

First Edition: 2013

mackids.com

This book is dedicated to my mom, Rheta, who, with
love and a whole lot of patience, taught me all things are
possible and encouraged me to follow my dreams; to my
daughter, Charlie, who warms my heart with her beautiful
smile and is making me a better person; and to my wife,
Jodi, who shows me every day what a best friend
and partner truly means. I feel so blessed.

—M. W.

Dedicated to the dreamers,
my third-grade students.

—L. S.

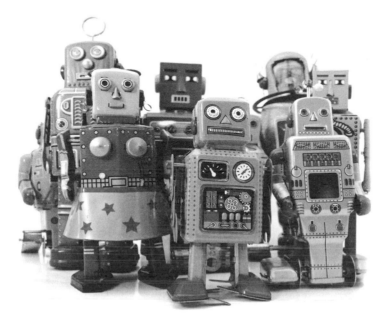

CONTENTS

A Word from the Creator 1

Chapter One **WHAT'S A KID PICKER?** 7

Kid Picker Profile: Austin .10

Chapter Two **GETTING STARTED** 13

Kid Picker Profile: Colt 28

Chapter Three **PICKING WITH A PURPOSE** . .31

Kid Picker Profile: Hannah 40

Chapter Four **EVERY PICK HAS A STORY** . . .43

Kid Picker Profile: Jonah 54

Chapter Five **UNLOCKING YOUR PAST** 57

Kid Picker Profile: Preston 70

Chapter Six **RUSTY GOLD** 73

Kid Picker Profile: Will .84

Chapter Seven **PICKER'S STYLE** **87**

Kid Picker Profile: Chloeparis **96**

My Picker Farewell **99**

Kid Picker Vignettes **101**

Photo Credits **107**

Acknowledgments **109**

Index **110**

MIKE WOLFE

AMERICAN PICKER

MY NAME IS MIKE WOLFE. I've been picking through junk ever since I was a kid. There's simply nothing that excites me more.

As a kid, my room was filled with all sorts of rusty relics I'd found while wandering through the woods behind my house. I loved collecting old comic books, plastic soldiers, monster models, and anything related to Evel Knievel (the American motorcycle daredevil

of my time). But the thing I loved to collect most was bicycles. I collected all and any I could get my hands on, from rusted relics that could barely turn their wheels, to 1960s banana seats, I loved them all. I'd often ride my newfound "picked" bikes down to an old junkyard or venture down the river just to see what caught my eye. I never quite knew what I was looking for, but that's what kept me searching, the excitement of uncovering those forgotten items of the past.

Some of my favorite childhood memories were of an old neighbor who lived down the alley from my house. He would let me dig through his garage, a place filled to the rafters with busted-up bicycles, old motor parts, and boxes upon boxes of tools. I once

MY FIRST 5 PICKS

1. 1960s BANANA SEAT BIKE
2. AN OLD CIGAR BOX
3. A BOX OF COMIC BOOKS
4. AN OLD MONSTER MODEL SET
5. SOME PLASTIC SOLDIERS

remember finding one hundred STP (motor oil company) stickers, and using them as my first trading currency for other items I wanted. To a wide-eyed young "picker" like myself, this was the next best thing to paradise.

If I happened across a rusted-out hull of a car, I'd search through the glove box looking for old registration slips, tickets, or matchbooks with advertising on them—anything that might tell the story of the owner or how the car came to find its resting place there in the weeds. My imagination ran wild. I guess you could say that's when I found my calling as a picker. I never thought of it as junk. To me, this was treasure.

My passion only grew with time. My love for bicycles led to opening a bike shop in Iowa during my twenties, followed by years of selling my found items to antique dealers and in flea markets across the Midwest. Never in my wildest dreams as a young boy searching though piles of rust could I have thought I would be lucky enough to not only make a living selling rediscovered junk, but to have my own television show, *American Pickers*. I'm proof that even your wildest dreams can come true when you do what you love.

Now I want to pass my passion for the great American tradition of exploring, collecting, and trading to another generation of kids.

THIS IS . . .

Kid Pickers

Chapter One

WHAT'S A KID PICKER?

BY SIMPLY PICKING UP THIS BOOK, chances are you're probably a "picker" at heart, just like me. You've got a passion for rediscovering those once-forgotten items of our past, and the stories they tell. You love the excitement of hunting through old items, or those that were tossed aside to collect dust. You understand their importance because you picked it, and you've begun a new chapter in the life of your picked item . . . now, that's cool.

So let's forget about what something's worth, or what everyone else around you likes. It's time to create your own story; find your own Passion. That's right, put on some old jeans, grab a flashlight, and set out for the journey that lies ahead. The adventure is all about

finding—picking—items that will connect you closer to yourself and the people that surround you. Whether these items have been cherished in your family for centuries or you've uncovered a rusty broken wheel in your backyard, the point is it's your pick and that's what makes you a true Kid Picker.

As a seasoned picker myself, trust me when I say you've got all the tools you'll need just by going out and finding what you like. My favorite memories as a Kid Picker were those in which I was the leader of my own journey, going out in search of whatever caught my eye. Curiosity will be your best guide (and, of course, this wonderful book you're holding), as you are now the creator of your very own picking story. Join me by following the guidelines in the chapters ahead on searching, finding, collecting, sharing, and creating your own story. Your journey awaits, fellow Kid Pickers. What will your story be?

Austin

AGE 10

COLLECTS: Bottles, rockets, old toys

BEST PICK SO FAR: Old bottles found
while digging in the dirt near
his grandfather's shop

Chapter Two

GETTING STARTED

A HOW-TO GUIDE ON WHERE TO FIND THE NEXT HIDDEN TREASURE

BEFORE YOU SET OUT into the world of picking, there are a few basics you'll need to know to get the best finds. And if you're like most beginning Kid Pickers, you probably don't have much in the piggy bank. No need to worry! The best picks you'll find will probably amount to the change found under your parents' couch, or your weekly allowance. But to be the very best Kid Picker in your neighborhood, you'll need to know where to look

for the next best find. (And ask permission from your parents, too!)

Have a look at my list of the best picking places to explore, and if you're really interested, why not start your own neighborhood picker club? (Just make sure you're the boss!) Besides, picking in a group is much safer, and a whole lot more fun.

MY PICKING POINTER:

Picking in a group is one of the best ways to pick. Two sets of eyes are always better than one.

THE BEST PLACES TO PICK

1 Your Neighborhood Garage Sales

I love scouring the newspaper for the next best pick. Start looking in your local paper, or simply keep your eyes peeled for signs advertising **YARD SALE**, **GARAGE SALE**, or even better yet, **MOVING SALE**. A moving sale usually means people have stuff they want to get rid of, which amounts to more items to pick from and better prices. Be prepared to use your *bargaining* skills. But I'll let the one and only Mr. PICKtionary tell you more about what it really means to bargain.

Presenting

MR. PICKTIONARY

(the "official" picker dictionary) for all your reference needs!

BARGAINING—Bargaining means that you're negotiating with the seller to get the very best price. Say you find an old box of G.I. Joe action figures, priced at $2.00 each. This is where you will use your bargaining skills to offer to buy three G.I. Joe figures for $5. It's a win-win situation! The seller is happy to get rid of unwanted items, and you saved a few bucks by using a bit of confidence and some bargaining techniques.

MY PICKING POINTER:

Don't be afraid to bargain down prices wherever you pick. Nine times out of ten you'll get a better deal, and heck, all you had to do was ask!

2 Secondhand Stores (aka Thrift Stores)

Secondhand what . . . you say? You know the places where your family donates items they don't want anymore? Well, that is exactly where you should hunt for the treasures that other people thought were merely junk, too. Some of my favorite undiscovered finds at secondhand stores are old board

games and books. I love finding really old books and looking inside the covers, since people often wrote in them with old inkwell pens to tell who previously owned it, or wrote an

inscription if it was a gift. It's great to imagine who may have owned it before. And board games are fun just because you can remind your parents how old they are. Take a look below at some of the secondhand stores you may have heard of and that may be in your area:

- **Goodwill Industries**
- **St. Vincent de Paul Thrift Stores**
- **Salvation Army**
- **Arc Thrift Stores**

3 The Auction!

Place your bids, Kid Pickers. Auctions are some of my favorite places to pick! An auction is not only going to be filled with interesting people from your town, but more importantly a wide assortment of unwanted stuff—the perfect place for a beginning picker. At an auction, an item or multiple items are offered up for bidding, with the highest bidder "winning" the item. You'll have to listen closely, as the auctioneer will likely be the fastest talker you've ever heard (it takes some time to get used to). Check out the list below for a few things to remember before you start bidding:

- **You will need to go with an adult who can sign up for an ID number that you can bid with (don't worry, it doesn't cost anything to register).**

- Try to get to an auction early, so you can look at what you are bidding on. (Don't forget to look under all those boxes, or any place other people may have looked over, since this is where you may find the best deals.)

- **KNOW WHAT YOU ARE BIDDING ON!** I'm serious about this, Kid Pickers. Auction life can be quite fast paced, so make sure you know the item you want to bid on and the limit of what you want to spend. I guarantee you, Mom or Dad will not be too happy if you spend more than you have, and you will be stuck mowing Aunt Cindy's lawn for the next three summers. . . .

4 Antique Stores

I'm sure you're familiar with them. Antique stores are sometimes old, often disorganized, and well . . . let's be honest, a bit smelly. Although they may be pricier than thrift stores or flea markets, there's always a chance of finding something that even the antique dealers have overlooked. Good dealers are history experts (it's what they do for a living), so if an item

catches your eye—ask about it.
I guarantee you'll leave with
some interesting facts and
hopefully an item you've
picked. So get to work with
that kid charm of yours, and
don't forget to talk down prices.
Let them know you mean business.

5 Flea Markets

Did you just say what I think you said? Fleas, as in those pesky things that bite animals (including your favorite dog, Knuckles)? Well, technically, I did say "flea," but this type of flea refers to a place where people bring items to sell. *Flea markets* can be held outdoors, but often you will find them set up in an old building, warehouse, or even your school gymnasium! Flea markets are a great place

to bargain with people. I like to think of them as *really* big garage sales with all different types of people and things. So check out your local paper, or search the Internet for local areas your parents may be willing to drive you to.

If you're wondering where such a name like **"FLEA MARKET"** came to be, the term actually originated from European street markets where vendors sold many second-hand goods—so many that they were thought to gather fleas!

Colt

AGE 10

COLLECTS: Old cars (including Matchbox), Lincoln Logs and other old building logs, old toys

BEST PICK SO FAR: Old Ferris wheel toy and old car toy bought at flea market

Chapter Three

PICKING WITH A PURPOSE

WHY PICKING IS NOT ONLY FUN, BUT GREEN (GOOD FOR PLANET EARTH!)

IT'S A SAD TRUTH, my fellow Kid Pickers, but the average person (yes—that means you) throws away almost 1,460 pounds of trash every single year. But by simply being a picker and reusing items, *you* can make a difference. I'm proof that saving the earth can be a lot of fun. Who knows, you might even end up making a living out of it someday!

If you're asking yourself what picking has to do with saving the earth, think about it:

Every time you choose to use something that was once considered trash (or items others no longer have a use for), you are *reusing* them, or in picker terminology, *repurposing*. Put simply, repurposing means making use of something again; what was once considered old, is . . . new again.

Think of yourself as a "treasure rescuer."
Every time you use an item no longer considered worthy or valuable, you are finding a
new home for something that may have ended
up in a garbage dump or been lost forever. Not
only is it wasteful to trash useful items, but it
adds to the problem of finding more space for
our landfills. That is why it is so important to
find the *creativity* within yourself, to see old
items in a new way. Take a look at some more
reasons why it's cool to repurpose:

The not-so-glamorous definition of a **LANDFILL** is what we usually call a "garbage dump." Landfills are generally built on low, flat land, where layers upon layers of trash are separated by clay, some type of lining, and soil, so as to keep as much harmful stuff from leaking into the soil as possible. (You don't want garbage juice to end up in your drinking water.)

Your History Rocks

Every item you pick has a story, or history, all to itself. That is what makes each item so unique. Close your eyes and imagine the life your item had before you. Think of the child who once played with an old toy (maybe your parents or grandparents owned it), or all of the adventures

an old bicycle has seen. The more wear and tear an item has, the more it's been loved, just like an old teddy bear found tucked away under boxes: It may be missing an eye or two, but it only means it was once cherished. The point is—use your imagination and curiosity to find out the rest (and read on about history in Chapter Four). The possibilities are endless. Just think of all the cool things waiting to be uncovered and appreciated by a creative Kid Picker like you.

Your Item Is Unique

Being unique means being one of a kind, and whatever treasure you make is your own; no two will be the same. Look at the years of wear and tear as added style points—heck, no one else will have the exact same one, right?

So if you feel like collecting old soda bottles and making your room into a 1950s soda parlor . . . then do it. No one ever stood out in a crowd by doing what everyone else was doing.

MY PICKING POINTER:

Perfection is boring in my eyes. I'd pick a pair of vintage jeans any day over any new pair found in a store. Worn jeans have a history . . . and that's cool.

You Save Money

Who doesn't want to save money? I can assure you, your parents will agree, too (college is expensive!). When you don't have to use the earth's natural resources to make a new item you would buy at the store, you most likely will not have to pay as much for it, either. Many of the items you pick won't even cost you a thing, since you're repurposing something that someone may have tossed in the trash pile. That makes *cents*!

Hannah

AGE 11

COLLECTS: Jewelry, old pots and pewter items, old tools, Radio Flyer sleds, wind chimes, small glasses, all things metal

BEST PICK SO FAR: Old tires that were resold to a used-tire wholesaler

Chapter Four

EVERY PICK HAS A STORY

DISCOVERING THE HISTORY AND STORIES BEHIND YOUR FOUND ITEMS

WHAT MAKES A GOOD STORY?

Have you ever found an old family photograph tucked away under boxes? Or discovered a letter written long ago? These *artifacts* tell a story, not only of when and where you found it, but more importantly about who may have made it or owned it before you. Think about what the person was like who owned it before it arrived in your hands. How old do you think the object is? Where did it come from? The true excitement lies in the mystery behind the items you pick, and I *love* history. It's unlikely you'll find out *all* there is to know about your object, and that's what makes the journey truly rewarding; use your imagination to fill in the rest.

When you pick, you're likely to come across a wide assortment of **ARTIFACTS.** An artifact is a man-made (yes . . . made by a human) object that has a particular use. So if *somebody* made it, it's an artifact.

WHERE TO BEGIN?

Since I'm sure most of you have heard of the movie *Star Wars*, let's pretend you bought a totally awesome Star Wars lunch box at a neighbor's garage sale a few weeks ago. Score! You've found an item and now what? How old is it? Who may have been the previous owner? How much is it worth? Where do I find more information on other Star Wars collectibles? Check out the list on the following pages for some great ways to find the history behind your pick.

THE LIBRARY

With thousands, and I mean literally thousands, of books about Star Wars memorabilia, you're sure to find at least one at your local library that could give you some information on your latest pick. And if you're lucky, you may even find a book on collectible lunch boxes alone (there are several to choose from).

THE INTERNET

Type in the keywords "star wars" (in quotation marks) on a popular computer search engine like Google and you will find literally millions of hits covering everything there is to know about the topic (in fact, more than 170 million Star Wars hits, in case you were wondering). The only problem is, that is an overwhelming number. And more than likely you'll have trouble finding any information on your mysterious Star Wars lunch box. Have no fear! An easy way to search for any item you pick is to look it up on eBay or Amazon (Web sites where you can buy and sell items). You'll not only find your Star Wars lunch box, but you'll also find out some history behind your pick, and how much it is selling for. Keep in mind, be as *specific* as possible about the item you are searching for. Type in as many keywords as you can about the item you are researching, such as "1970s Star Wars vintage lunch box with thermos," otherwise you may be overwhelmed with hits.

MY PICKING POINTER:

Beware of what you read on the Internet, since often not all the information is factual. So, play it safe and double-check your facts in a book on the topic. Visit your local library for help.

PEOPLE
THAT'S RIGHT, ASK AROUND!

Didn't you say you found your lunch box at a local garage sale? Well, what are you waiting for? Go back to your neighbors' house and ask them about your item. Chances are they have a story behind it, and would love to share it with you. What you pick says a lot about the person you are, and when you venture out in your community to learn more, you're connecting to your roots (there's no place like home). Every community has interesting characters with stories to tell; it's your job to find them and make certain they are never forgotten. Besides, I love talking to people firsthand about where items come from—I learn something every time and it's often a total surprise.

Who knows? You might find out that twenty years ago your lunch box was

owned by a boy who used it every day for lunch throughout elementary school. I guarantee you won't find that information on the Internet or at the library! Your item now has a new sense of value because you know how much someone used it and loved it before you became a part of its history. Continue your picking journey, and maybe repurpose it to a once-again functioning lunch box. Who knows—you may start a new trend at school by having the first cool vintage lunch box.

Jonah

AGE 9

COLLECTS: Rusty metal, old artifacts, antique toys, old pieces and parts

BEST PICK SO FAR: All of it. "You can't throw away history!"

Chapter Five

UNLOCKING YOUR PAST

THE MOST IMPORTANT DAY OF YOUR LIFE: THE ADVENTURES BEHIND ANCESTRY

YOU MAY HAVE ALREADY guessed it . . . but, yes, the most important day of your life was the day you were born. Prior to that day, the world unfortunately didn't have the chance to meet you. Okay, so what? What does that have to do with anything? We all love our birthdays because we get presents (trust me . . . I was once your age, too), but the true gift of being born is that you are now a *new* part of your family tree, connecting all the wonderful traits and talents that make you one of a kind in a world of over 7 *billion* people . . . and counting.

KID PICKER = DETECTIVE

Being a Kid Picker is all about unlocking the mysteries of our past. Any time you start to sort through old items and artifacts, particularly family items, you are taking on the role of a detective. Asking good questions is the first step in becoming a master detective. If you really think about the things you love in life, too, you may find it has something to do with the family you were born into! The things you love may not seem like such a coincidence once you dig into your family's past. You love Star Wars items? Maybe one of your older relatives was also a fan of the early *Star Wars* movies, or even the old TV show *Star Trek*. Cool, right? As a Kid Picker looking at all the generations of your family, you won't believe what unfolds in front of you.

Your **GENES** are exactly what makes you unique, since each and every person has a specific genetic makeup. Genes hold our DNA (genetic instructions) that tells what traits will be passed on to the next generation.

LET THE JOURNEY BEGIN

That's right, your journey starts *today*. Around your home you'll find artifacts that tell the world not only about the things your family likes, but also about the items that are *important* to your family. So . . . start searching or, more importantly, start asking the right people. That means not just your parents, but your aunts, uncles, cousins, grandparents . . . maybe even your elderly neighbors who may know a lot about the people in your town, including your family!

STEP 1 Picking an Item

There are many different family artifacts you could choose to learn more about, such as a family quilt, diary entries, handmade cards, a locket your grandmother always wore, or any medals or certificates that mark family achievements. The list is endless; it comes down to how much you are willing to search and how *clever* you will be about your search. Think of what lies hidden in boxes and

drawers, or in a family chest kept in the attic. Remember, think outside your family home, too; you should have several close relatives who would love to share their stories of these treasured pieces of the past with you. And be sure to ask permission before looking through your relatives' personal items.

STEP 2 Asking the Right Questions

Let's start out by assuming that an easy thing to find would be an old family photograph. Say you've always wondered about that picture of your grandfather Eli that is framed above your fireplace. He is pictured atop a small horse, and you, too, love horses. Now take a closer look at the photograph, and start asking questions. Have a look at the following example:

KID PICKER DETECTIVE QUESTION LIST

1. How old was my grandfather when this picture was taken?

2. Did he own this horse?

3. When did he and his family immigrate to America? (If so, from what country?)

4. What was his full name? *(You may even be named after him!)*

5. What did his family do to earn a living?

MY PICKING POINTER:

I suggest you start documenting all the information you will be gathering. It could be as simple as writing in your very own *Kid Picker Ancestry Journal* or videotaping your grandparents or other family members as they recall your family's history. The point is—whatever items or information you come across may not be of any monetary value to the rest of the world, yet to you they are priceless. Your history is a part of you; it's the story of how you came to be.

STEP 3 · A Closer Look

So, you've picked some family objects to learn more about, and you've talked to your relatives . . . now what? If you're willing to do a little more detective work, you won't regret the mysteries that may unfold, being the clever Kid Picker you are. There is a wealth of information literally at your fingertips, so take a look at a few more options below if you're up to the challenge:

The Internet

Just as in Chapter Four where you learned about researching an item, you can also find links to your ancestors. Just beware that many of the

Web sites you'll find charge you for access (such as Ancestry.com). But if your parents are willing to pay, or you've saved up enough birthday money . . . you're in luck. There are also Web sites that are 100 percent free, but you may have to navigate and spend a bit more time to find information. Check out the USGenWeb Project at www.usgenweb .org for more information (again, it's a *free* Web site).

Your Local Historian

As long as your town is bigger than one block, there is a good chance that it will have a local town historian or, even better, a historical society that is dedicated to helping interested people like you on the great ancestry hunt! Bring in your artifacts (family items) and a list of questions. You may not find all the answers, so use your imagination to decide the rest. Make it your own story.

The Graveyard

Yes—you heard me right—the cemetery. A little creepy, I know, but actually cemeteries are a great place to find ancestors you were unaware of. It was common for people to be buried next to other family members. (Unfortunately, many children and adults died at far younger ages years ago due to the lack of advancements in medicine we have today.) Ask your parents and family members if they happen to know where any of your relatives were buried. Search out those graves, pay your respects, and look closely at the surrounding graves. You may find names of people both you and your family never knew existed. Write those names down, and travel back to your local historian.

Preston

AGE 11

COLLECTS: Antique tins and signs, old fishing gear, World War II items, anything unusual

BEST PICK SO FAR: Antique Thomas Edison lightbulb and World War II aviator hat and goggles

Chapter Six

RUSTY GOLD

HOW MUCH IS YOUR PICK WORTH?

DOES IT HAVE TO BE RUSTY...OR GOLD?

Your item absolutely does not have to be rusty or gold. I've been digging in junk piles since I was a kid, finding forgotten items that to most people were of no value, but to a treasure hunter like myself—they were my "rusty gold." These items *do not* have to be dirty, rusty, gold, or even old, for that matter. But they do have to be something that interests *you*. Once you decide you like an item, that's when it becomes your *rusty gold*.

WHAT ABOUT REALLY STRIKING GOLD?

FINDING SOMETHING THAT'S WORTH A LOT OF MONEY!

Let's get this straight . . . there is a chance that you could come across something that's worth a lot of money (and we'll get more into big money items later), but, more importantly, the items you pick will have a personal value all their own—worth more than what's on a price tag. Take a look at the next page to find out more about the value of an item.

INDIVIDUAL VALUE—Your own *personal* value of the object. The enjoyment you get simply from owning it, not how much money it is worth.

MONETARY VALUE—How much money your item is worth. This is where you put a real price tag on something you picked.

Monetary Value!
(or More About the Moolah)

There are three important things you need to know before you consider how much an item is worth. Take a look at the following list, and don't forget to ask questions about any item you may be picking. It *never* hurts to ask.

RARITY

We're not talking about how well done you want your steak tonight, we're talking about how *rare* the item is you picked. The harder an item is to find, the *rarer* it is. Pick something that is rare *and* that many people want—the price will be higher. Pick something common that not too many people want—the price will be lower.

A SHORT LESSON ON ECONOMICS FROM OUR FRIENDS SUPPLY AND DEMAND

(A) Pick something that is rare *and* that many people want = HIGH PRICE

(B) Pick something that is common that few people want = LOW PRICE

Keep in mind your item does not have to be old to be rare. Since we love lunch boxes so much, check out an example of a rare pick below.

A RARE FIND

You've hit the Kid Picker jackpot and scored a 1950s Annie Oakley lunch box at a local yard sale—awesome! What makes this particular pick rare (besides being old and in working condition) is that it includes the original thermos. Most lunch boxes from this era have since lost their thermos friends! Happen to pick this item with the thermos; you've picked something worth upward of $750–$1,000! Most lunch boxes you find won't be worth $1,000 (more like $10), but remember it's not about the dollar signs here, it's about picking what you like!

2 CONDITION

What kind of shape is your item in? An item in "rough" condition shows all the signs of age, or wear and tear. For example, a teddy bear in rough condition would be missing its button eyes, and maybe an arm or two . . . you get the picture. On the flip side, an item that is nearly in perfect condition, or "mint," looks as though it's never been touched. Pretend ol' Teddy the Bear is in mint condition this time, and as you may have guessed, all his parts are together *and* he's still in

the original box he came in! So, when considering the value of something—condition does matter. Take a look at the following examples for the importance of condition when picking an item.

READER BEWARE: YOU ARE NOW ENTERING THE ANNUAL STAR TREK CONVENTION!

Imagine it—you are attending a Star Trek convention—everyone is dressed as a favorite character from this classic TV show. You come across a table of vendors selling action figures and notice similar Mr. Spock action figures from 1974: One is in the box (M.I.B) and the other is not. Like I said, condition affects the value of your item.

M.I.B.

M.I.B.??? Yes, a very good term to understand, especially when you do your research on eBay to find out the value of an item. M.I.B. refers to "mint in box," almost-perfect to perfect condition. This means your item will be worth more money than an item in rough condition, or without the original box. Average price for our friend Mr. Spock M.I.B.: about $100.

N.I.B.

Okay, there really is no such term N.I.B. (not in box), until now, I guess, but you get the picture. Here our friend Mr. Spock is missing the original box and also a few accessories that came with the original action figure. A true Star Trek fanatic might pass on this item, simply based on its condition. Average price for this guy: about $10.

How old is the item you picked? Most collectors consider "antique" items to be at least seventy-five to a hundred years old. Keep in mind what I said before; it's all about the *experience* behind your pick, and going on a treasure hunt to discover something *you* like. Items can still be of value to you (whether personal or

monetary) even if they are not considered antiques. Take for instance, our action figure, Mr. Spock: Although this item is not seventy-five to a hundred years old or more, it's still worth a good chunk of change (M.I.B.). However, often the older and rarer an item, the more valuable it is.

MY PICKING POINTER:

Make pickin' a family outing and learn something about your parents you never knew before. Perfection in any item is boring. So don't think about dollar signs when you pick, just go out and have fun with it.

Will

AGE 8

COLLECTS: Old signs, wheels, car tags, anything old!

BEST PICK SO FAR: Antique farm tools

Chapter Seven

PICKER'S STYLE

DECKING OUT YOUR ROOM WITH RUSTY GOLD RELICS

SO YOU'VE ALREADY EARNED lots of "cool" points for starting your own Picker Club, searching for rusty gold, unlocking your ancestry, recycling, and starting lunch box trends at school, but what the heck do you do with the rest of this stuff now?

Here's where all the cool things you've picked start to form a bigger picture. Now you get to use your creativity as a picker to start designing or repurposing all the items you've discovered. I'm asking you to think outside the box here. There are tons of different ways to use or repurpose an item that's 100 percent absolutely your own unique idea.

PICKER PARADISE CHECKLIST

A GUIDE TO CREATING THE COOLEST BEDROOM IN YOUR NEIGHBORHOOD

Get Inspired

First off, pick one item you've found that seems to stand out more than the rest. Look at the item more closely and ask yourself the following questions:

1. What was the original purpose of this item?

2. Could I use this item for a different purpose?

3. How could I change this item, or make it even more unique by adding my own details?

4. Could it become wall art?

5. Could I design a theme for a bedroom based on this one piece?

If you've answered yes to more than one of the questions on the previous page, then chances are you are off to a good start for some great bedroom design ideas.

Make It a Family Project

Connect with your parents' found items and passions. Often you don't have to look any further than Dad's collection of train memorabilia in the basement to discover you, too, think it's pretty cool. Maybe this will become the new bedroom theme for your room. Start by asking your parents and family members not only what they are interested in now, but also what they liked when they  were kids. Once you've got some ideas, go out and treasure hunt with your family. I promise it will be fun . . . just don't fight over which radio station to play when you're riding in the car (Mom always wins).

MY PICKING POINTER:

You don't have to spend a lot of money (or *any* for that matter) to create a space that represents you. Just look for things you like!

Find a Bedroom You Like ... and Copy It!

I don't mean literally copy it, since it would be difficult to find exactly the same items as another kid picker's. But seeing other picker paradises that interest you is a great way to inspire ideas for your own room's theme. Take a look at the examples below. Often it only takes one unique piece to create your own paradise.

VINTAGE PARADISE

The focal point of this room is based on a vintage children's advertisement poster. I think this is a Kid Picker score, since chances are you won't find another like it; remember: Standing out from the crowd is a good thing! Take a closer look and you'll find other cool vintage items, like a child's kitchen set and an antique bed frame.

So what makes something *vintage*? A vintage item does not have to be as old as an antique item (one we would consider to be about seventy-five years old or more). *Vintage* simply refers to a particular item from a specific era—for example, a *vintage* 80s dress or a 70s lunch box. As long as it was made before you were born, it's considered vintage.

REPURPOSING PARADISE

Here is a great example of getting creative with the items you find to design a room. An old hardware store display rack is now *repurposed* to make a bedroom bookshelf. To add more interest, an old wagon wheel has been turned into wall art and used school lockers have been repainted for storage—*sweet*! (And good for our friend planet Earth, too!)

A COLLECTOR'S PARADISE

Find your passion, collect items that represent it, and *display* your collection! You can collect anything, and I mean literally ANYTHING. This Kid Picker happens to be an animal lover (in case you can't tell). Find whatever it is that interests you and show it off. Who knows how many stuffed puppies you will have in fifty years!!

Chloeparis

AGE 8

COLLECTS: Original Cabbage Patch Kids dolls, old mini toy cars, old Barbies, old clocks

BEST PICK SO FAR: Old Singer® sewing machine purchased at a flea market

MY PICKER FAREWELL

Picking is all about connecting to the person you are and the people in your life. It's about that moment when you uncover something that's been lost in a junk heap and know that you like it. It doesn't matter what anyone else thinks—it's your own *unique* pick. To the next generation of Pickers, I wish you the best of luck in your adventures ahead. If I leave saying one thing, it's that I hope I've sparked your imagination enough to inspire a lifelong passion.

Sincerely,
Your Picker,
Mike Wolfe

BASEBALL CARDS

—The T206 Honus Wagner card from 1909 sold in 2007 for a record $2.8 million. Talk about hitting a Picker home run!

Honus-Wagner.org "Honus Wagner T206 Price and Owner History" (2008). http://www.honus-wagner.org/2008/02/honus-wagner-t206-price-and-owner.html

YO-YO'S

—Chico, California, is home to the National Yo-Yo Museum, where you will find the world's largest "working" wooden yo-yo, weighing in at a whopping 256 pounds!

The National Yo-Yo Museum Web site (2010). http://nationalyoyo.org/

BARBIE—Since Barbie's first introduction in 1959, she has had more than 100 different careers, from astronaut to Olympian, and over forty-three pets (including a chimpanzee)!

Jones, Abigail. "The Ultimate Career Woman." Forbes. 2 March 2009. http://www.forbes.com/2009/03/05/barbie-careers -jobs-business_resume.html

MARBLES—The official term for someone who plays marbles is "mibster" (not to be confused with "mobster").

Gold, Ashley. "Bloomfield Mibster Brings Home the Marbles Crown." *Pittsburgh Tribune-Review* on the Web. 25 June 2010. http://www.pittsburghlive.com/x/pittsburghtrib/news/ pittsburgh/s_687577.html

JEWELRY—In Roman times, many men wore jewelry as a symbol of status.

Mirza, Sumair and Jason Tsang. "Rome Exposed— Roman Life" (2011). http://www.classicsunveiled .com/romel/html/clothmen.html

LEGO—Did you know LEGO™ is the number-one tire manufacturer in the world? Though tiny, they produce 306 million rubber tires a year!

"The Making of . . . a LEGO" *Bloomberg Business Week*. 29 November 2006. http://www.businessweek.com/bwdaily/dnflash/content/nov2006/db20061127_153826.htm

OLD BOOKS—The most expensive book ever sold, at $30.8 million, was Leonardo da Vinci's *Codex Leicester* (though it's more like a notebook). If you're wondering who the lucky bidder was, that would be Bill Gates.

Reynolds, Christopher and Hugh Hart. "Da Vinci Codex" *Los Angeles Times*. 15 January 2007. http://articles.latimes.com/2007/jan/15/entertainment/et-hammer15

LICENSE PLATES—During World War II, states conserved metal and made license plates from recycled materials. Some used a soybean-based fiberboard—but that was discontinued after goats found them tasty. Seriously!

"Illinois License Plates." Syracuse University Special Collections Research Center (2012). http://plastics.syr.edu/featured/license_plates.php

TEDDY BEARS—The teddy bear was named after the twenty-sixth U.S. president, Theodore "Teddy" Roosevelt.

Mullins, Linda. *The Teddy Bear Men: Theodore Roosevelt & Clifford Berryman, Historical Guide for Collectors.* Hobby House Press, Inc, Cumberland, Maryland, 1987.

STAMP COLLECTING — The most popular U.S. postage stamp ever sold was of the one and only Elvis Presley, selling more than 120 million copies.

"Don't step on his blue suede shoes. Elvis remains the king of stamps." *USA Today* on the Web. 26 December 2006. http://www.usatoday.com/money/2006-12-26-stamps_x.htm

LUNCH BOXES — During the 1970s in Florida, metal lunch boxes were actually banned for a time, fearing that some children would use them as playground weapons. Yikes!

Bellis, Mary. "Metal Lunchbox History" 2012. About.com http://inventors.about.com/library/inventors/bllunchbox.htm

BICYCLES—Before bicycles with pedals and cranks were invented in the nineteenth century, they were made of wood and moved along by kicking on the ground. Basically, a two-wheeled scooter with an uncomfortable seat!

"A Quick History of Bicycles." Pedaling History Bicycle Museum. http://www.pedalinghistory.com/PHhistory.html

PHOTO CREDITS

There are many print and online resources to collectibles such as baseball cards, vintage toys, and action figures available from your local bookstore or library if you'd like to learn more about specific items or categories that interest you. And of course, you can ask your family, your neighbors, and even your local museum staff about items you "pick" at home or in your town. The many items shown throughout the book are intended to inspire you, and do not necessarily represent items from the authors' personal collections or from the television show *American Pickers*. What do you think the stories are behind the photos?

All photos courtesy of www.shutterstock.com except: pp. x, 2, 93, and 95: courtesy of Mike Wolfe; p. 77: courtesy of iStockPhoto. All Kid Picker Profile photos courtesy of Kid Pickers' families.

ACKNOWLEDGMENTS

I want to thank all those who have made this book possible: My coauthor Lily Sprengelmeyer, Nancy Dubuc of AETV, Simon Greene and Rosie Bilow of CAA, Jean Feiwel and Liz Szabla at Macmillan Publishing, Kim Gilmore of HISTORY, the crew at Cineflex Productions, my brother Robbie and sister Beth, my neighbors who let me pick their garage, Marty, Bruce, and Alex in Leiper's Fork, Tennessee, my childhood friends in Bettendorf, Iowa, and the glue from start to finish, Bill Kamper.

Most of all, I want to thank all the parents, teachers, and Kid Pickers who have inspired me to pass on the tradition of picking to another generation.

INDEX

A

American Pickers, 5

Ancestry (see Family history)

Ancestry.com, 66

Antique stores, 23–24

Artifacts

   definition, 45

   family, 61, 67

Auctions, 21, 22

B

Barbie, 102

Bargaining, how–to, 17

Baseball cards, 101

Bedroom (decorating

   with picks), 92–95

Bicycles, 2–4, 106

Bidding (at auctions), 21–22

Books (vintage), 19, 103

C

Condition (of items), 78–80

E

Evel Knievel, 1

F

Family history, 35, 57–69, 90

Family tree, 58

Flea markets, 25–27

G

Garage sales, 16

G.I. Joe action figures, 17

Graveyards, 68–69

H

History

   community, 51–53

   family (see Family history)

   of picked items, 45

   reseaching tools, 46–53

I

Internet (as research tool),

   48–50, 65–66

J

Jeans (vintage), 38

Jewelry, 61, 102

Journaling picks, 64

K

Kid Picker definition, 7–9
Kid Picker profiles
   Austin, 10–11
   Choleparis, 96–97
   Colt, 28–29
   Hannah, 41–42
   Jonah, 54–55
   Preston, 70–71
   Will, 84–85
Kid Picker safety, 14

L

Landfill, 34
LEGO, 103
Libraries (as research tool),
   46, 50
License plates, 104
Lunch boxes (vintage), 45, 49,
   52–53, 77, 105

M

Marbles, 102
"Mint in box," 80, 82
Moving sales
   (see Garage sales)

N

"Not in box," 80

P

Photographs (family), 63
Picker Club (starting), 87
Posters (vintage), 92

R

Rarity (of items), 76–77
Recycling, 31–34, 39, 88–89, 94
Repurposing (see Recycling)
"Rusty gold," 73–74, 87

S

Secondhand stores
   (see Thrift stores)
Stamp collecting, 105

T

Teddy bears, 36, 78–79, 104
Thrift stores, 19, 20

U

USGenWeb Project, 66

V

Value, of items, 75–83

Y

Yard sales (see Garage sales)
Yo–yo's, 101

Tamara Boots Holden

LILY SPRENGELMEYER

is a graduate of the University of Iowa and a third-grade elementary school teacher. She has been a lifelong picker, growing up in her father's eclectic antique store called La Belle Epoque in Galena, Illinois. Mike Wolfe was a regular in her dad's antique store; she and Mike met as young Kid Pickers. She recalls often talking with him about their shared passion for old bicycles.

Sprengelmeyer's best childhood pick was at the age of five, when a two-dollar set of earrings caught her eye. Later, her father came to find out that they were Victorian gold earrings worth several hundred dollars. She still loves to repurpose vintage items into "upcycled" clothing and accessories, and often paints pictures from old photographs that inspire her. Sprengelmeyer resides once again in Galena, Illinois.

THANK YOU FOR READING THIS
FEIWEL AND FRIENDS BOOK.
THE FRIENDS WHO MADE

POSSIBLE ARE LISTED BELOW

JEAN FEIWEL, *Publisher*

LIZ SZABLA, *Editor-in-Chief*

RICH DEAS, *Creative Director*

HOLLY WEST, *Assistant to the Publisher*

DAVE BARRETT, *Managing Editor*

NICOLE LIEBOWITZ MOULAISON, *Production Manager*

LAUREN BURNIAC, *Associate Editor*

ANNA ROBERTO, *Assistant Editor*

FIND OUT MORE ABOUT OUR AUTHORS AND ARTISTS AND OUR FUTURE PUBLISHING AT MACKIDS.COM.

Our books are friends for life